BIRCHMERE

ANDREW LIVINGSTON BOYD

WestBow
PRESS®
A DIVISION OF THOMAS NELSON
& ZONDERVAN

WestBow Press books may be ordered through booksellers or by contacting:

WestBow Press
A Division of Thomas Nelson & Zondervan
1663 Liberty Drive
Bloomington, IN 47403
www.westbowpress.com
844-714-3454

Cover designed by DesignOnTop Studio.

ISBN: 978-1-6642-1932-8 (sc)
ISBN: 978-1-6642-1933-5 (e)

Library of Congress Control Number: 2021902209

Print information available on the last page.

WestBow Press rev. date: 2/15/2021

To my beloved children

CONTENTS

INTRODUCTION

Maybe you are like me. Maybe you found yourself on one of life's unexpected highways, with no clear destination in mind. Maybe the other drivers are unforgiving; they honk their horns loudly and make unpleasant hand gestures towards you. So you pull over at the next convenient stop to gather yourself.

Birchmere was my convenient stop. My refuge. A place to catch my breath.

Between 2015 and when I moved to Birchmere Close, my marriage failed. A business venture was unsuccessful. I was separated from the two girls I adore and who adore me. My best man was killed violently in a community from which we escaped. Another friend was slain in an adjoining neighbourhood within the same year. I lost almost everything I owned - except my mind and I sometimes wonder why it kept hanging around the way it did. Those tumultuous years gave me more than enough fodder to chew on. Consequently, in 2017, I started putting on paper whatever moved me.

On January 17, 2019, I discovered the famous American poet, Mary Oliver. Yes, we met the day she died and I couldn't have enough of her. I bought a few of her books and immersed myself in her world.

By the time I moved to Birchmere Close in June 2019,

Mary (we are now on first name basis!) had opened my eyes and ears. The quietness of Birchmere spoke to me loudly. Its lake, teeming with scaled and feathered lives, stirred me immensely. I began to see poems in almost everything that moves, breathe, dies and others that sit still, minding their own business. That's when this book was born.

But be warned, I have never studied creative writing or Shakespeare. (I actually googled the spelling of his name to write this!) I am a numbers speaker who hold qualifications in Chemical Engineering Technology and Physics. And even though my vocabulary now includes free verse, I am not supposed to be a poet. Bear that in mind as you read my thoughts on family, friendships, love, loss and nature.

So, like me, maybe you need to pull over at the next convenient stop. Maybe this book is that stop. Maybe you will aim to catch at least your breath and catch the rest of your life!

BIRCHMERE

All the tall trees
Look on in admiration;
have you noticed,

how they bow their heads
in your direction,
shed teary-eyed leaves all year?

Do you wonder why
they sing you praises,
shelter the lives
kneeling at your feet?

Well, you've got a way
with me too;
I'll give you that—
you've got a way with me.

SUNDAY MORNING

It occurs to me how blessed
the morning was—
the sun was shining,
the air was filled with the songs
of a bird choir
and the sound of dry leaves
under the hurried feet
of a gray squirrel—
when it appeared out of nowhere,
a presence so compelling,
I searched among the new clothes
of the nearby trees for its source.
And there she was:
a dark green goddess
of small yellow petals.
She was confident and comfortable
and standing
next to an old park bench.
And what could be more beautiful?
I do not even know her name.
Still, I took her away with me:
a fragrance lingering
long after
I said goodbye to the lake.

PEONY

Peony, what is the word
for the way bees find you,
the way they put their fine lips
to your pink cups,
the way they stumble away
half-heartedly,
drunk on whatever you have to offer?
Irresistible?
Yes! Irresistible!

TO THE BLACKBIRD IN MY FRIEND'S BACKYARD

To the blackbird
in my friend's backyard,
the one who flew
from the cold fence
to the wet grass,
the one who landed softly,
head tilted, beak ready:
it's winter,
but I notice the weather
did not deter you.
So I hope you find
what you are looking for.
I hope within
the bent blades
of the green grass,
fate holds
something wonderful
and worthy
and kind enough
to your patience.
I hope you keep
the spring already in your step
and that you may even
dance a little to fresh hope
wiggling between your beaks.
But if not,

and the world continues
to be unkind,
know that it is acceptable
to lose one's spirit sometimes,
for disappointment
is just another
pair of wings to fly with.

EAVESDROPPING

Lots of things have opinions,
even birds.
So maybe the doves
cooing in the backyard
this morning
were having an early disagreement
over something significant
and necessary
and worthy of my attention.
So I listened
but kept my distance
like we all should
in matters of this nature.

ANYTHING WORTH THINKING ABOUT IS WORTH WRITING ABOUT

These days, I collect experiences.

I go as far back as my childhood
or as near
as the next conversation
to find a good one;

then I wrap them in words
like I'm trying to do now
and hope they will be remembered.

MYSTERIES

There are mysteries
in this world
warmer
than summer
and smaller
and as gentle
as a soft kiss
and so mysterious
we cannot
touch them,
but they touch us
even so,
like the thing in me
that's quite aware
of you
and feels right.

THE LITTLE WORKER ANTS

The world that tried to recruit me
has a thirst for things
that cannot be quenched,
and it's not prepared
to work like ants to get them.

I like ants.
Ants are optimistic
and diligent.

The little worker ant
lives three years—if that many—
and all the range of her life,
she fills the two stomachs
of her body
with food for the colony
and herself.

But does she think,
even for a moment,
of hoarding
when her whole body
was made to be selfless?
I don't think so.

So maybe we need
the life expectancy of ants;
maybe two stomachs
and a small body
would give us their perspective
on living, on things.

DRAGONFLIES

They are not as common as bees,
but every now and then
on mornings like this,
one would cross the water
toward me.
Its eyes, large and luminous,
seem to belong to a body
not so slender
and much more complicated.
But they are beautiful,
so I observe them with much care
and oh Lord, God of amazement,
they do testify—
the way they hover,
then are gone—
the way their frail wings
speak of something wonderful,
something much greater
than the lift
they so effortlessly provide,
never leaves me.

THE COOT (I)

Every day I walk beside you,
I prepare myself to be dazzled.
Today, it came from the bushes
in front of me:
a small frame dressed
in a sleek black coat.
It wobbled along on weird feet
and as if on a catwalk—
and why not?
Aren't we all models
in our own right,
walking the runways of this life?

THE COOT (II)

Canada geese and coots
are common here,
but the coots are brave,
and sometimes,
one would swim
to the edge of the water
to greet me.
Once, a gray chick stopped and gazed
from the most curious eyes
I've ever seen on a bird.
So magical it was.
So enviously clothed
in a body that floats
just above the water.
It must have felt
the touch of my own curiosity;
startled, it quickly crossed
the sleepy water
without breaking
so much as a ripple.

LESSONS

There are lessons to be learned
from grass huddling
in the October morning cold.
I urge you,
ask the ones with spikes of seeds
to mark their age;
ask the ones with none.

DEAD FOXES

It's not the first time I've seen you
in a lone lane
of a not-so-busy highway,

and it's not the first time
I've seen your reddish-brown fur
flung backward,
your flesh, the secret it kept
beautifully in life,
now exposed for all to see.

But do not think for a moment
I did not hear you cry
as you reach for the scraps
in the bin below my window,

the way I hear your body
cries now
to be laid in a nearby field.

THE PRODIGAL SON

Have you ever seen anything
as beautiful as trees,
in the phases of their lives,
standing and waving their branches
in unison?
And would it have occurred to you
that a blackbird with its white breast,
sitting easy on a low branch
of a gray bark tree,
would sing such melody
to mark the moment?
Well, I wouldn't.
And neither would I have imagined
that the lake would lie in silence,
awed by the way they greeted me
that evening,
much like the prodigal son.

THE LONGING (I)

It's been a while since my last visit,
darling lake,
and even the coot may have forgotten
the amazement in my eyes
as I watched her strutting along
your loose-barked runway
in her sleek black coat.
But I am not the coot,
so except for the mornings
rising from the eyes
of my daughters,
you do not have to guess
for whom my heart longs daily.
Oh darling lake,
how can I resist you any longer?
This life—even with its busyness—
has robbed me of some small
but very significant things,
the latest of which is you.

THE LONGING (II)

Every day at dusk,
I long to see the wind
crossing your waters toward me.
And every day it does,
along with ripples
from the feet of ducks.
You entice me
with her majesty the goose,
calm, white-coated, so stately
on her lofty throne of blue,
shimmering crystals
and with the bulrush
standing at your deep edge
like guards with thin, green blades.
But I do not have to visit to be blessed,
darling lake;
wherever I am,
I only have to think of you,
ears tuned, eyes wide opened,
heart humbly bowed.

SATURDAY MORNINGS

Saturday mornings
are ripe for walking,
for freeing the lungs
of all the week's concerns.
I find I can claim the promises
on the young, unbiased air
with each step,
hold them firmly
with each breath I take
of the Saturday morning air.

If You Could
Read My Mind

If you could read my mind,
you'd see yourself
the way I see you—

not like tulips
whose pretty faces
are always there
to welcome spring

or the sparrowhawk
so elegantly perched
on a low branch
above the garden.

No.

But like an oak tree
wears the years with grace—
how beautiful it stands,
how imperfectly
beautiful its soul!

EVENING AT THE LAKE

Given it was late evening,
I was delighted to see the sun
still sending you
her warm approval,

and even the lilies lounging
in the shallows of your water
were smiling broadly
in utter amazement.

And if they, sweet lake,
as beautiful as they are,
can stand in awe of you,
how can I resist?

THE CIRCLE

The sign read "no fishing,"
but it stood knee-deep in the water,
beak wet with entitlement,
so I guess it ignored the sign
and went fishing anyway.

And oh, darling lake,
how difficult it must be
to be a silent witness to this:
the way one life ends
so another may live,
and over and over again,

and how unfortunate it is today
to be the fish caught between
silent pleas for mercy
and the gratitude of a hungry stork.

PROVIDER

You will not tire, it seems,
of making me smile,
nor will the plum trees
at your water's edge grow weary.
So you must be delighted, surely,
to be so loved and so admired.
And why not?
You are blessed with the smiles
of the souls
that come to you
to be watered, to be fed,
and to be whole once more.

Some Decisions

I don't want to get this wrong,
so I prefer to hold on
like maples do.
I read that in the autumn,
they are one of the last
to let go of their leaves.
They choose instead
to go from green to yellow
and then to orange or red
while waiting on winter
to make up her mind.
I don't blame them entirely,
for some decisions
should not be rushed,
so I guess I'll take my time
and mellow
just like maple leaves.

CHERRY PLUMS

The tall trees and the long grass
were deep in conversation,
and I listened,
for it was all talk about you.
It's hard, they say, to keep the secret
along your western border a secret,
and the sky agreed,
and the heavens opened,
and I was drenched
in childlike enthusiasm.
So I asked the blackberries
to grant me safe passage
through the undergrowth,
and they did,
so I made my way
about three meters in,
and there, just above my head,
were cherry plums
waiting to be plucked, to be eaten,
to be a juicy part of my story.

ONE QUESTION

Who fluffs the pillow
of the sleepy-eyed evening,
kisses her glassy forehead
before she sleeps?

UNDER THE WEATHER

Except for the waves
rippling across your body,
you were rather calm this morning.
Often, we are like this:
thoughtful and reflective,
so utterly consumed
by this thing or that thing.
But what concerns a body
of near-still water?
Maybe the sky knows;
it too is home to birds and trees.
But if the gloom
hanging over your waters
is just you being under the weather,
understand this:
we too can be like this sometimes.

YOU CALLED ALL AFTERNOON

You called all afternoon,
and I answered,
and there you were,
frolicking with ducks, fishes—
all the brave creatures of your waters—
while the sun kept watch
from the balcony of the sky.
The fishes—some bream, some pike—
dipped in and out of the water,
splashing your cool happiness
into the warm face of the evening.
So pleasing it was to see
your wild and youthful side awaken,
so pleasing to watch
you throw yourself into
the dance with early summer.

GOODNIGHT

You are not the deep blue pavement
Jesus walked on.
Neither do you rise and fall
with the kind of joy
oceans are known to have.
But this evening, the way the sunlight
settles on your shoulders,
the way you shimmer with delight
as you comfort the last of Sunday,
the way you were not distracted
by duck calls, crickets—
all the sweet voices heralding the evening—
fills me with such happiness,
and I'm so glad to have met you.
So sweet dreams,
sweet lake, sweet dreams.

THIS MORNING

This morning, the tall trees
were unexpectedly
in a good mood;
their branches swayed coolly,
their leaves flickered with such delight.

But below them, squatting
above the gray concrete,
their thin leaf cousins
did not share their excitement.
It seems joy can only be found
in winds high above their heads.

Aren't we the lucky ones,
we who find happiness
at any height above the ground?

I'VE KEPT THE SMILE

I've kept the smile you wore
on the day we met.
It's in a gift box
on the table
next to my heart
and sits on a white cushion
steeped in admiration.
I could not think
of a better place
to preserve
my first impression of you,
lest I forget
like we tend to do sometimes.

WHEN I DIE

When I die, scatter me
across a meadow.

Divide my ashes
among the daisies, ants—
anything that'd have me—
so they wouldn't have to cast lots.

I want to be a reason
the wild grass puts on
its lush green coat once more

and the reason bluebell
lifts her face
to the sky and rings,

and if the brown earth
is so inclined,
I'd love to be the reason
she breathes
a thousand breaths.

So do not confine me
to a lonely room
beneath the ground.
I beg you,
take me high above the heads
of some tall trees;
release me to the wind.

Out Strolling
with Friends

About two hundred meters
from the backyard,
down a mulchy slope
and into the leafy shadows
of the tall trees,
I saw the first patch
of intense purple heads.
They were held up
by green, slender shoulders
with succulent leaves for hands.
Our tour guide, unofficial
but knowledgeable,
said these woods
are partly protected
because of them.
Then the bluebells call out.
"Come closer," they say.
"Breathe me."
And I went closer and breathed
and breathed and breathed.

DEAR MUSE

When our chats
were like cherry blossoms,
our poems were pink
or white and tender.
I long to write like that again.

Smoke Signals

You may think this an act
of utter desperation,
but come tomorrow,
I'll climb to the top
of the tallest building
I can find and make myself a fire.
I intend to send up smoke
heavy with the things
I have to say but my mouth
is forbidden to deliver—
and this, I think,
is the best way to do it.
So whatever it is I'm feeling,
I'll put it into the open air
for her to read,
and tomorrow is as good
a day as any to start.

DAFFODILS

Some say the climate
has gone emotional
and this is the reason.
But you can tell by the way
they sometimes enter the world—
purple heads at home
above new snow—
that they are simply brave.
I much prefer this perspective
and will keep it.

ROOM

In my mind, where everyone
has a compartment,
yours is brightly lit
and warm enough
to hold the way I feel.
And in the event I forget—
even for a moment—
why I feel like this,
I can unlock the door,
make myself remember.

FOR WHAT IT'S WORTH

For what it's worth,
I think about our chats
when I'm away
from the screen and you.
Recently,
one made me smile
so hard, a colleague
asked if I was okay,
which made me laugh
the way I do at jokes
only you and I find funny.
I wanted to say,
"I'm in love, and I'm sure of it."
But instead, "I'm fine"
were the only words
brave enough to leave my mouth.
The truth remained silent until now.

ISLAND GIRL

When the beach calls,
each grain of white sand
silently screaming my name,

I do not need the palms
to convince me;

I stop what I am doing,

whatever it is I'm doing,

and listen,

for I'm an island girl.

COMFORTING MY MOTHER

Mother, those flowers are from
the first man who said he loved you.
They're fresh enough to remember
when the day was too short to hold him,
so you moved him to the moon,
worshiped him from a distance.

But Mother, your arms are aching.
Nobody told you
regret could be this heavy,
that a smile to light a thousand stars
could bring the worst of winters.

So Mother, be soft with yourself,
for someday, the sun
will convince another moon
to smile for only you.

COME TO THINK OF IT

Come to think of it,
there's a place between
when I last saw you
and when we next meet
that shares a border
with excitement,
and the air is reckless here—
like a mild summer—
and anticipation paints pictures
with my thoughts of you
across a sky eager
to carry our dreams.
Forget-me-not
blooms all year round,
dresses daily in your smile,
and vows to keep the twinkle
in my eyes alive
until we meet next.

AFTER RAIN

After rain, when rivulets cease
to make their way
across the yard

and the last crystal beads fall
from the burdened sweetsop tree,

after the sun cracks
its first
flirtatious smile

and flattered earth
emits a scented moan,
the misty magic begins.

JOEL

When I heard the news about Joel,
I recalled how to weep
for someone who's not family.

I met Joel one September
at the foot of a journey whose head
we were both too short to see,
and he greeted me
with carefully weighed words
and a smile that tried
to keep his teeth a secret.

Within a year, our school moved
from a building ripe with history
into a collection of concrete boxes
bejewelled with glass and
an amphitheater at its centre.

In some ways, the lone oak
in the orchestra reminded me of Joel:
his towering intellect,
the sturdy friendships he formed—
some rooted in the God
he later came to question—
and skin hard enough
to bear the brunt
of their teenage burdens.

I used to think only cowards do
what Joel did,
but this was his second attempt.
The first time, life clung to him—
like it did at birth—
and he just couldn't shake it off
the way he was able to do this time
with just enough help from hopelessness.

THE WAY WE LOVE

By the age of twelve,
you learn to build a dam
to hold the salt water inside.
For men do not cry
or tell their sons they love them
in a language their ears understand.
So each time I awaken
to homemade pancakes,
crispy bacon, oddly shaped
fried eggs from him,
each time he taps me
on the shoulder,
releases a half-smile
as he moves between his
bedroom and the kitchen,
I hear him say, "I love you, Dad"
from the top
of his seventeen-year-old lungs,
and I reply, "Thank you, my son"
from the bottom of my heart.

Notes

Birchmere is a Park located in South East London.